DATE DUE			

The Dogwood Tree

Alabama Poetry Series

General Editors: Robin Behn and Thomas Rabbitt

The Dogwood Tree

Jennifer Atkinson

The University of Alabama Press
Tuscaloosa and London

Copyright © 1990 by
The University of Alabama Press
Tuscaloosa, Alabama 35487–0380
All rights reserved
Manufactured in the United States of America

The paper on which this book is printed meets the minimum requirements
of American National Standard for Information Science-Permanence of
Paper for Printed Library Materials, ANSI A39.48–1984.

Library of Congress Cataloging-in-Publication Data
Atkinson, Jennifer, 1955-
    The dogwood tree / Jennifer Atkinson.
      p. cm. -- (Alabama poetry series)
    ISBN 0-8173-0487-8 (alk. paper). -- ISBN 0-8173-0488-6 (pbk. :
alk. paper)
    I. Title. II. Series.
PS3551.T57D6 1990   89-20454
811'.54--dc20   CIP

British Library Cataloguing-in-Publication Data available

For Clare
and as always, Eric, to you

Acknowledgments

Grateful acknowledgment is made to the following publications in which some of these poems first appeared:

Boston Literary Review
  On Courtesy
Cincinnati Poetry Review
  Birds of the Air
  Chestnut Blight
  Daughters of Jerusalem
  For Love of Nina Ruth
  The Words Would Have Us
Delmar
  An Exercise in Ambition
  On the Nature of Things
Fine Madness
  His Pleasure
Gulf Coast
  Nor Wishes
  To Save the Blooming
Poetry
  Afterward
  Choosing Happiness
  The Dogwood Tree
  Fortunetelling
  Hail on Stone Mountain
  The Magic Words
  Philosophy Class
The Reaper
  On Courtesy
River Styx
  Prosperity

Sonora Review
  Exposures
  Jephthah's Daughter
  Magdalen's Passion
  Near
  Rehearsal
  Resolution

"Rain" is reprinted from *Prairie Schooner*, by permission of University of Nebraska Press.

And special thanks to *The Pushcart Prize XIII* (*1988-89*) in which "The Dogwood Tree" was reprinted.

Contents

The Dogwood Tree

The Words Would Have Us

Blame the veer for the hawk,
      The hiss for the sour apple;
Blame coil for slack,
      Judgment for dusk & rattle;
Blame skitter on pride,
      Swoop on swindle & stagger;
Blame blood on luster,
      Trust on blue thistle & brine;
But praise the tense of the curse
      For the green, sibilant course
      Of promises & history—
Fleece, foil, mystery.

I

The Dogwood Tree

Mown once at midsummer, the field
has taken months to recover
its half-wild hodgepodge of color—
the shades now of early fall.
From the window, she can guess at
what grows there. The purple must
be joe-pye weed, the yellow tufts
would be goldenrod. That red
bush is a blueberry, that blue
spire a cedar. She hasn't
been moved to walk down there all year—
among the briars and broken
stalks—to find the small lives
distance obscures. But in the center
of the field there's a dogwood tree,
as straight and perfectly round
as a child would draw it. The leaves
have gone red, and the berries,
past ripe, are now wine. She can tell
by the birds. A whole flock of
something black—grackles or starlings—
has descended to feast on
the fruit. It happens every year.
And every year the birds fall,
drunken from the hidden branches,
easy, almost willing prey.
This year she would like to touch one,
open its vulnerable
wings in her hands, feel its talons,
its fear, the glare of its black,
yellow-rimmed eye. And she would like
to return the bird unharmed
to the ground where it fell, reeling,
close to what she might call joy.

An Exercise in Ambition

Under the auspices (albeit
leafless) of a single fifty-foot oak,
one particular tree whose haggard,
deciduous silences unnerved
her, the tree toward which her rambling walks
eventually led, she felt compelled
somehow to speak, to say something true
unwaveringly and with eloquence,
as if there beside the tree
upon the frozen, adamant earth
somehow the language itself would come
to her rescue, she would testify,
and something like justice would be served.
But, of course, she never spoke. She stood
waiting under the stark, Romanesque
architecture of the branches. Words
failed her every time. Overhead, crows
shook out their black glove-leather wings and
cawed whatever crows will caw. A pine
sapling, pungent and straight, let the wind
say what the wind, in its wisdom, would.
That's all, she thought, there's nothing to it.

Dominion

I'll never forget
the birch trees chalked white
against the hemlocks,
how the mint birch sap
sweetens their leafless
March twigs, how lichen
climbs their bent, damp trunks
in summer, and rot,
the August woods' true
work, starts in the white
flesh of the weakest
trees. I always loved
the slim birch. But out
beyond the fire-cleared,
scrub blueberry fields,
out where the woods go
nearly wild, I felt,
as a girl, a right
to full dominion.
I'd look for decay-
cored birches, the ones
woodpeckers rifled
and ants colonized,
and I'd shoulder those
defenseless birches
down. It was easy.
But I loved them just
the same.
      One winter
day an ice storm hit,
sealing all the woods
under its brilliant,
icy weight. I could
hear the trees breaking—
the split-wood crack, then
the jangle of limbs

falling. Like plate glass.
But the birch was arced
across the firepath,
its tip pinned, its trunk
bowed too taut to stand
the strain long. I broke
what ice I could and
eased the treetop from
the iced-over ground.
Suddenly the birch
pulled itself free. Ice
rang against ice. I
shut my eyes, listened,
and it seemed the whole
woods broke loose of me.

Sky Shows Around the Edges

The leafless trees and the leaf-strewn, ulterior
thawing woods—catbrier, lichen, and the elsewhere-scarce
    candelabra
ground pine—all that and the laurel glassy with rain.

Test that green and the lustrous planes of the hemlock against
the dangled plumb bob of a single word.

Near

for my mother

Three deer hesitate beyond the laurel but finally do come into the clearing. We let them gnaw our apple trees and newly planted spruces. We talk of growing beans outside the garden just for them. We need them near us.

Grazing nervously across the lawn, the deer stray in closer to the house. We turn off lights to admire their knobby legs, cowlicked flanks, and white-tufted ears, stiff now in awareness of us.

We will them to trust and to stay. They startle, freeze, but then don't run.

I remember trundling out a basket of winey apples one long ice-stormy winter. I dreamt that night of hooves cut on snowcrust, my footsteps full of blood. I knew the apples were no gift.

But we need the deer to come up close like this. We need them to look so skinny and easily hurt—so much at our mercy that a fierce tenderness completes us.

We've stalked the deer back through the blueberry fields, taking paths marked with their heart-shaped hooves. Sometimes the dogs find antlers half-buried in fern or snow. We collect them. We love to touch the blunt end, rough where it touched the deer's live flesh. We want to know.

Once, holding the frozen, hacked-off leg some jacker had thrown aside, I waited for the melting blood to ooze, real into my hands.

Later we found the secret place under the hemlocks, where the warmth and weight of half a dozen deer had pressed the grass and ground pine down as they slept the night before.

10

But we didn't huddle in or wait. We turned away. Enough that they are so near.

Rehearsal

Summer nights she'd draw up her knees and smoke naked in the dark. From the bedroom doorway where I'd stand to wish her good night across the room, I'd see only the smoke-white skin of her legs, the red circle of her cigarette. I'd have to imagine a face.

Her face—behind the words of best wishes, pleasant dreams. But those good dreams take practice.

One morning I told her I'd heard someone screaming No in the night. I didn't say I thought it was her. "But, Jen," she said, "it was you. *You* were screaming in the night."

Today, on my 29th birthday, I put on her old cotton dress. It almost fits. Already I feel my body growing pale beneath the cloth. The buttons cold fingers down my back. The mirror. A fan fills the room with wings. Her dress flaps against my legs as if it hung empty on the line to dry.

I used to watch her hang out the wash, the whole heavy basket steaming, neighbors waving from the next yard. I remember her laughing with those friends—a joke about bloody sheets, weddings, and chickens. I knew I should understand. I knew it was all about love and lies, a sad joke she'd try to keep me from. Though she knew all I wanted was to laugh.

I overheard stories of her childhood—the lobsterboats, the series of mutts, the first proud drunk, the first baseman she loved in high school—and learned them all like the words to a song. Rehearsing.

You are your mother's daughter, they said.

In the dream it's always summer, and she, with pearls wound chill about her throat, is 19 and practicing engagement, envisioning the white stiff shirt and unambiguous black cummerbund of the bridegroom. I know this. She wears this white dress. The wind with this white dress insinuates the beautiful edges of her body.

She is picking wild blueberries. Fruit rings her pail like bursts of rain. The hem of her dress, as she strains to a top branch, tilts across the fields. I want to tell her.

I want to say *hurry* or *stop* or *I'm sorry*. But she cannot hear me. I am not here. And already she turns. Already, knee-deep in lupine and wild snapdragons, she heads home, walking, kicking up moths—clouds—the anise dust, pollen, ash of goldenrod.

Philosophy Class

Across the way, a neighbor's ornamental
tree fumes with hazy blossoms. Gray
and barely rose, they're almost bodiless,
a blur trapped in a weir of branches:
smoke tree. And stuck in my head the silly words
Where there's smoke there's fire, an argument
for the existence of God, I'm sure, but
the reason for this smoke is sex.
In philosophy class at seventeen, I hardly
listened to all that talk of a somehow unmoved
mover, first cause, the one who wound up the world.
Engrossed instead in harder evidence gouged
in the desk before me, I would lay my paper
across the wood and shade it over black
with even strokes—a technique learned on gravestones—
until the image reappeared in white:
G.P. (perhaps) *& Christy*, and *Fuck you*,
Call 314-0134, and hearts,
Grant sucks, et cetera, the testaments
of love. And like a medieval scribe's
fair copy of Aquinas, illuminated, here
with scrolling and the fine grotesquerie
of a genital marginalia.
                              To reach the night
classroom I had to cross an unlit, unused
"A" parking lot where just a month before
a woman had been stabbed, they said, first
then raped and left dead in the bushes.
I wondered how they knew which happened first,
but I wasn't scared. All huddled up
in my bulky parka, furred hood drawn down low,
what little beauty I owned well cloaked,
I thought my body was securely shapeless,
that beauty caused desire, desire rape.
So rape, I reasoned, crossing the dark, was theft,
as in a Tibetan Buddhist tale I'd read

in which all this hybrid world was born
of just a moment's want. Enough in Paradise
was getting dull, perhaps, and so to break
the pattern, theft. Call it greed, desire,
sin, excessive love, and yet in the tale
there's no talk of blame or motive.
The only question Buddha always would
refuse to answer was *What happened first?*
Because it's a waste of time to wonder.
What matters is what happens now and next,
the narrative (and how to break its spell.)
                                        Smoke

tree blossoms have no scent, no beauty,
except as a whole cloud of delicate
color. No one bloom there is worth stealing.
But the lowest branch last night was torn, it looks
like deliberately, off and hangs by just the tough
greenwood bark, not worth the bringing home.

Back in Philo 101, our dark-eyed, young
professor smoked a pipe he never lit,
resisting all temptation, rubbed his chalky palms
clean along his blue-jeaned thighs. *Ah, beauty,*
he admonished, *has been variously
defined. Imagine a cave . . . shadows . . . a perfect
circle, purely mind.* But all of us
and he knew very well who was the beauty
in the room. He dared not look at her. I stared
and prayed for dangerous looks like that.
                                    Our professor

and the woman never spoke. While he
imagined caves and counted causes backwards,
she doodled elaborate crosses twined with flowers
and words from the board like *ergo, first,* and *saint.*
I know because I watched her. As I watched
her run across the empty parking lot
twice a week when philosophy class let out.
And as she disappeared in the dark and trees,
I listened hard for her clacking shoes, afraid

for both of us. Before finals she stopped
attending, and I'll never, of course, know why.

Chestnut Blight

Nothing is secret, she thinks, now,
listening from her attic bedroom
to slammed doors and then silence downstairs.
Outside, a thousand-geared machine,
the bees, works the two green domes
of her father's prized, young, European
chestnuts. They wear heavy
Victorian tassels of bloom whose scent
is so densely sweet she can taste it.
Not more than a few true American
chestnut trees stand now,
already faltering with the native blight.
She was taken once to the hill
at Devil's Den Park to view them,
emblems of her parents' youth, but now
she can't recall the look of blight.
Were the trees black? Cold but charred
as the mealy-fleshed roast chestnuts
city vendors sell from their pushcarts
at Christmas? Were they leafless? Bare?
Without shade and hollow? All
she remembers is the litter of husks,
spiny, dangerous underfoot, and red
squirrels chirping, furious but distant,
a music like the low, throaty,
birdlike chirps a cat will affect
to lure her prey into ambush.

Afterward

I walked in up to my waist
and the skirts of my blue party dress lay
themselves open there on the surface, held
as if in midair like a dancer's.
I walked in deeper. Step by step
the lake claimed my arms and ribs,
my breasts, my shoulders,
neck and chin, lips, and then the whole
weight began to lift. My body, as always,
would support me. Deaf in the lapping
summer water, I lay on my back,
dress and all, just watching
those reliable stars,
those hot, distant stars.

Resolution

It was full-on summer.
Miller moths hung thick in the air.
Under a wild persimmon tree, the dropped
rotting fruit steamed with flies and yellow jackets.
And the fox—its brush—the easy way it dallied
across a fallen log, looked back, leapt
into the high red grass, and vanished.

Fire in fire.
At least that's how I remember it this morning.
Alone last night I couldn't sleep.
I listened to the furnace kicking on
and off, I read and dozed, back and forth
between the Samson story and half-dream.
The tale starts foreshadowed with angels and fire,
Samson is born. A chapter later, his wedding.
There are complications: a narrow escape,
a riddle, threats, and a love scene, but finally
—as I knew she must—the bride betrayed him.
Afraid of Samson's anger, she ran
and hid alone in a stone hut.
Mud wasps whirred in the walls' rough chinks.
The story doesn't say how long she stared
up the aisle of ripening wheat
that led straight from the smudged horizon
right down through her open door.

The text
in Judges says only that "Samson
went and took three hundred foxes,
and took firebrands and turned tail
to tail, and put a firebrand in the midst
between two tails." In passion Samson torched
three hundred foxes then chased them
down the hill. She saw the whole field
flaming. The smoke from the scorched grain. I knew
their story would end with her betrayal and his
revenge, but still the image haunts me: a fox

19

crazed, its body only pain and light,
lost in the fiery wheat and running hard
—not skulking—
                    straight for her as if for home.
Our story couldn't end so easily,
so dramatically. But God how I envy her
pure, live fear. I wish I had betrayed you.
One shared pain would be simple,
would finish and make our story whole.
But between us there was no clear
conflict and so, finally, no resolution.
Like that fox three years ago in the clearing
gone in the fox-colored grass before
I could raise my arm to point at where
it paused for that one pending moment.

Jephthah's Daughter

Already two months alone.
Twice no blood.
Anyone who sees me now will know.
Under their leaves our grapes grow heavy.
The gourds loll back on the fence,
bitter with too much sun.
I soak my dress, doze until it dries
or the goats start their milking-time whimpers.
So much solitude is dangerous.
This silent heart is relentless as logic.
If he doesn't return
then I am a widow in virgins' colors,
the elders will choose me a husband,
my husband will call me a whore,
and I will be stoned in the marketplace.
If he does come home
he will be king, the elders
will give him a bride,
the elders will choose me a husband,
my husband will call me a whore,
my father will kill him and steal his land,
I am a widow in a blood-stained shawl.

The Magic Words

And he took the damsel
by the hand, and said unto her,
Talitha cumi.

1
A half-moon half-lights the furrows
where mustard—green, good, bitter—
has suddenly burst into trivial bloom.
The rest of the garden, too,
grows past ripe.
Snailshells glint in the dirt.

Only the onions survive this heat.
Sometimes, since water is scarce,
I spit along the row,
staining the ground
dark around them. But
they would live without my care.

Kneeling, I can smell the onions in the earth.
The fringe of their leaves is cool
along my wrist as I feel for the bulge
of the fruit from the bed—
white fruit I refuse to harvest
all at once, as I should, into garlands.

Each night I yank up just one,
knock it clean against the ground
and bite straight into the clear core.
I don't repeat his magic words.
I bury the tasted onion
right back into the earth.

2
My father calls it miraculous.
But I no longer sleep, or even dream.
Done with the garden,
nights I wait out listening

to the dreams flying in and out,
in and out like dumb sparrows
through the open windows
of my parents' mouths.
Back in the dairyroom yesterday's curds,
wrung in bleached cheesecloth
and hung, drip down from their hooks
whey and whey and whey
into the wood catch-trough.
Sour countable rain.
Death was a rain.
It touched me everywhere.
The other, the one I must thank,
took only my hand and tugged.
Unable, unwilled, I stood.
My dress clung dank
to my back. He dropped my hand,
saw it fall against my thigh
and watched me breathe.
As if he could see me
under the cloth, under
the garment even of skin.
My parents on their knees mumbled
miracle, miracle, miracle
and refused to look as he tore
the braided sabbath loaf,
parted my lips and teeth with his fingers
and stuffed my mouth with bread.
As if I were a sick lamb balking
at its medicine. Forced,
I had to swallow. He left.

3
This body is dangerous.
Too perfect to touch.
Even my father backs off.
Every night he lies into his folded hands.
Grateful, I'm grateful,

and leaves me a pouch of coins.
But I've neither bought
nor given anything since my return.
The merchants will not barter
with one who's bargained with death.
Even the beggars stop their whining
when they see me coming.
Just once I tried to give.
The woman was blind, alone,
and maybe stupid.
I laid three heavy coins
across her palm and closed her fist.
At a safe distance,
the crowd ringed around us.
They expected her
to die at my touch, or at least,
transformed to suddenly see.
Dazzle or curse.
She sensed their nearness
and distracted, turned toward them,
and forgot to thank me.

II

Windy Easter Sunday

The shrug, the balk, the resignation—
we'll call it—of a Western Kansas wind is passed
from Woodlawn to glum awnings, red and wan,
striped and ripped, to lilacs,

whose hunched-up, burdened shoulders lift
and fall on the wind's who-knows.
What is April but the sift
of—hope, call it—pollen through a rashly opened window?

What is spring but another season bent
on passing, on phasing out its three full moons?
Yet the luck of the day is irresistible! Intent
on faith we dress for summer, for a church festooned

with Marian lilies. Sure enough the storm wind
stalls, caught—snagged, we might almost say—
on the Oxford Baptist steeple. Who cares? The hymn
begins. We stand and sing, "Jesus Christ is risen today."

Nor Wishes

As a girl
I worked at salting fish.
The woman beside me split
and opened the bodies
like sealed imperial letters,
tore the wasted contents loose,
and rinsed. I rubbed salt
into the ribbed, white meat,
salt into the glint-
green skin and gills.
Sometimes I spelled her
with the knife. Together
we layered up the fish
in barrels for sale in Jerusalem.
Salt-fish from Magdala, near Galilee,
from the waters of Lyre Lake.
After the salting days,
our hands and arms stung
where the fins had chafed
and salt and scales ground in.
Washing off, she joked and teased
about how long our salted
flesh would keep, uncorrupted.
I'm not sure if then
—the fresh lake's waves
lapping at our black basalt shore,
wind-poppies a red blot
on the way toward Capernaum—
if then I understood her jokes.
But I laughed.
Later when she fell sick—
bad blood, they said—
I knew no salt, nothing white,

would preserve her. Nor wishes.
All there was was just
to hold her two hands,
her two hands.

Magdalen's Passion

He charged the air with a different dark.
This is night. I know night.
I can hear it in the disquiet
of early wind, the pigeons,
the scrape of the dung-collector's
shovel against the stone-paved square,
the door and the splash—a wine merchant
pouring out the last of the moldy lees.
When vinegar
           from the soaked sponge dripped
into his open mouth, I cringed
expecting to taste that sour with him,
expecting my sun-cracked lips to sting.
Yet I tasted wine—good, full wine.
The others, his friends, would call
my thirst, my fear, and my relief,
a wine-cooled tongue, treacherous.
Soon they will all turn away.
It will be as before, body
all I own, I am.
           Now I own grief.
This hollow body is poured half full
I can feel the heaviness move
inside the skin with every step.
My son, my daughter. Grief
is a worthy possession, and costly.
I have too this errand, this last
expense, his body.
           Though the light
is not yet pitched steep enough
to reach Jerusalem's narrow alleys,
here in the open market-square
it is nearly another morning.
Vendors unlatch their doors,
set out their wares. Men squat
to slurp cups of sugared mint tea.

Mothers joggle their babies quiet.
One woman, kneeling apart, cutting
squares of honeycomb,
                              starts
at a child's cry. The cloth
across her breast goes dark, damp.
And she is embarrassed.
Her husband must blame her
for their infant's death, and beat her.
The soles of her feet are grilled with welts.
Pain is teaching her body grief.
Like a fine string puppet's
                              her shoulders
shrug up and down as if sobbing,
but quiet. Gloved all in honey,
she will not cry: she cannot
touch even her own cheeks
to dry the tears. Besides, salt
would bitter all she owns.
Honey ribbons off her knife, slows,
drips back along the blade,
to fill again the cut wax combs,
and she returns to work,
                              as I must to mourning,
to buying sweet spice—rich myrrh,
fresh alocs, camphor, and oil—
to dress his emptied body.
I would like to pay too much.
But the spice merchant, cross-legged
among his heaps of saffron and crushed
cayenne, cinnamon
                              dust in the folds
of his robes, his hair, is honest
and insulted that I would scorn
the ceremony of his livelihood.
To honor him—the merchant—then,
I must dissemble, pretend to be
as clever as any man's wife
at buying her family's supper,

haggle hard over the worth
of spice-dust and oil, fragrant
balm for his now painless
wounds, marks of a horrible ingenuity,
cruelty his friends will soon call sacred.

Sanguinaria Canadensis

Models of decorum, false poppies,
but nothing like poppies' fire or drowse, the flowers
hold themselves so stiffly. Unburdened

by leaves or anything green, they're a wax
mockery of snow, and what else but the snow
and they can achieve such cold,

a cold I do not admire.
And yet I'll search the woods for them,
proof under the sleeping maples,

among the thaw-soaked, fallen basswood leaves
of the early-blooming plant called *bloodroot*.
The flowers would deny

that their stems and buried
roots are charged with a red
alkaline juice so bitter it protects

from touch, from grazing deer,
the eight white petals of their every bloom.
As a girl I wanted but was afraid

to stain my hands
red with a juice once used as war paint.
I am no longer afraid.

To Save the Blooming

peonies from the storm, I pick them,
fill jars, bowls, mugs, and glasses.
In every room I display the cut flowers.
Their beauty from a distance like a painting,
up close is rough strokes
of flush and cream,
fair flesh and blood tinges
of the color carnation,
which too is a flower, all
torn-edged petals and sexual heart, called
first dianthus as if for the virgin
archer and sometimes clove pink
for its fragrance—
Christmas spice and blooming—
a scent so compelling
my friend Anne who reads travel brochures
has dreams of walking Valencian fields
where carnations grow wild and crushed
underfoot freely give
up their perfume to the air.
But clove pink
—there is no turning away—
means also the nail through the palm
not, I think, of Christ but Francis
whose love of God, light, Clara
finally scarred even his flesh
with the stigma of passion.
His wounds must have been luxury
to bear through the long ordinary
hours of summer ease, his love
proven real as pain, as flesh and blood.
At nightfall when the storm begun
in the distance draws close,
I watch from the door.
The wind through the screens
stirs the sultry air full of sweet

flowers arranged in tap water,
hardly touched, kept safe,
denied the wind's damage.

On the Nature of Things

The painter chose the color umber.
Umber, a smoulder of earth and iron ore
(earth, even the untilled scraps of gone-wild ground
outside the gates, aches for motion: look how dust
invites the wind; and iron—magnetic, black—
too when visible reddens, gladly it seems,
like a maple tree in April: corrosion
the cost and color the profit of change),
is set down square as if it's a table. As if
a table could ever rest on a floor this
polished and unwobbly.
                                    Once upon a time
that umber and the matte, celestial blue raised
there at the lip and waist, neck, elliptical base,
fluted trim, and trapazoidal front of five
of the nine exemplar objects would have posed
the questions *ubi sunt?* and why ashes to
ashes to dust. Consider the Dutch version:
a half-gone glass of ale and oysters, shucked but uneaten—
the diner called away—a salt cellar placed
on the table to represent desire.
                                    However,
this large interior landscape
insists otherwise on changelessness and art
as an antidote to time. Just look at how
the decorative clover leaves are rendered blue.
Green would be inviolate among the things
revered here. But such insistence after all
when argued with urns, cup, umber, and sky
is an admission of all it would protest
against.
            Yes, it is true I love the abstract
valid syllogism doggedly contemplated here.

But what I know is the green, and underneath
me giving earth—the lie of the land—it would deny.

On William Bailey's
Large Umbrian Landscape,
a still life

On Courtesy

There is a story in the Midrash
glossing perhaps a text
where strangers turn out to be angels.
A man invites friends
to his son's wedding feast.

He cajoles the guests, fills their glasses,
sends his son back down to the cellar
for a rare vintage red.
The son is fatally bitten
by a snake coiled under the casks.

When the host hears, he says nothing.
Children dance in the doorway;
a girl licks date-honey
from her hands and hair.
He will not spoil the revelry and pleasure

of his guests till the time of toasting is over.
Then he apologizes for the inconvenience.
Yet the story I read is not of the man,
the son, the guests, but
the bride and how she takes the news.

Veiled in bleached gauze,
hands white
from rubbing them with lemon
daily all last month,
she thinks of her bedroom

curtains blowing in and out
on the summer wind,
the smell of tangerines,
the raw rice her mother poured
into a draw-string pouch this morning,

the price of her dress
and whether dye would disguise it,
that she should cry now
and cannot, but she must
so she thinks back.

Ten years ago her father said,
what a shame!
I always wanted a pretty
daughter, an angel.
And she weeps.

The tears are genuine.
All the guests are satisfied.

Expecting Fear

In May with a man I loved
and his friend whom I later married
there were lilacs and an open grave.
To prove myself I leapt in scoffing,
expecting fear, any sensation
of life, but it was nothing—
straight-cut dirt walls, sheered sod, and chance
wafts of the lilacs' purplish bloom.

A June bug larva lay on the bottom,
oily, translucent flesh curled up
dormant in its shell, its yellow husk.
I wanted to crush it
or to prod it alive,
the gold seal of its body broken,
but I was barefoot and
hadn't the nerve to touch it.

The earth kept crumbling in my hands
and underfoot as I tried to climb out.
The men stood back and laughed
out of sight to scare me, and it worked.
Finally palms, legs, face soiled,
I gave in and called. The man I later married
grabbed my hands and lifted me
free of that other's grave.

His Pleasure

Why do you stand so long at the lake?

Is it the space, the wide
ballroom of water, the glinting
polished floor?

Is it the wreck of summer,
the yellowed spikes of wild
iris, the snapped and tangled fish lines?

Is it the pine air at the shore,
cleansed of voices, my voice,
soft in its false patience?

I stood long at the lake as a girl.
Before I ever saw you.
It was the quiet I loved.

And the fish that dared
almost to touch
my foot, dangled in the water.

You do not dangle your foot in the water.
The trust of a lake trout,
the brush of its mouth and flicked tail,

does not interest you.
You just stand there in the morning
or any night there is a moon.

The house is lit or dark behind you.
And I—I think you know this—
kneel undressed at the window, watching.

Exposures

A thin farthing of ice sealed up
our garden pool this morning. The lilies
and your fancy mottled carp might well have frozen,
except that as I watched from upstairs,
the new kitchenmaid stepped out
hugging her wool coat close.
She trotted out the boiling teapot,
steam gusting around her sleeves, the slight
inadvertent spills melting a black-dotted path.
Pouring her silly kettleful
into our pool of Chinese goldfish,
she must have whispered endearments, prayers,
yet suddenly she looked up to my window,
aware, and ran like a thief for the house.
I wish I could say she lifted her skirts
and ran with a glad grace, showing
the hem of an eyelet petticoat,
but no. She fell, and her black-clothed
body lay for an instant still
among the icy formal beds, the prostrate
English thyme and frost-killed lavender.
Why must even a girl's romantic gesture
and her private, awkward fall seem an emblem?

That girl fallen against the frost
and bright sensation of winter
is the negative plate of an execution
I happened one evening to witness,
at a distance, of course, and by chance:
the hangman and the audience, correct in black
coats, hats in hand, and the guilty one,
against the dusk and dark horizon of the others,
already shrouded in white.
What orchestration. The body went limp
at the stroke of the hour.

And remember that wedding dance? Not ours,
but the one where we touched first as strangers?
The bride's house in the falling snow,
all the furniture stacked in the garden
to allow for three full sets of dancers.
I played fiddle and drank.
You danced, and once near the end, slipped
in a pool of spilled beer—mine. Ashamed,
you took my hand, stood, nodded politely,
and quickly continued the Allemande Left
or Right-hand Star, glaring.
It was at least an hour before
your skirts were dry and the dance done.
I played so trim and fast that night
I caught the bride's eye. Did you see her,
dressed for the memory's sake in lavender scent
and her mother's white dress, come kiss me
dead on the mouth? I thought it was thanks,
then, and joy. But today I see it was fear.
It was fear, my love, wasn't it fear?

                    after reading the notebooks
                    of Thomas Hardy

Hail on Stone Mountain

Bashōknew that hailstones simply
clatter on bare rock crags,
so rather than trudge another hour
uphill to listen and find the words
in the storm at the top,
he turned aside and returned
the wayside innkeeper's bow of invitation.
He settled down on the inn's
wood porch under the eaves
and fed his breakfast rice
grain by grain to the sparrows
who shared his refuge.
Their speckled breast feathers
riffled back in the cold wind.
One's wing hung bent.
He gave it no extra attention,
though the others kept it from eating.

His tea had long since
stopped steaming, forgotten
till a clink came of iron on iron:
the innkeeper's daughter stirring the fire.
He hoped she wouldn't shuffle out
smiling to offer more.
The way she held her head
to hide that bulging purple ear,
the fear and the gracefulness,
but especially her silence
(he guessed she was nearly deaf)
distracted him. It pulled his body from itself
and made longing seem falsely
easy to fill. He wondered
if she were always silent.

The hail whitened the garden rocks.
He thought of it falling

in the long dark rice furrows
already sowing next year's winter
or pummeling down the first
plum blossoms, their scent broken
open like jars of cloves and honey.
He thought of the girl's body stung
with its hard, cold points.

He flicked another rice grain out,
then dumped the whole bowl.
Claws and beaks clicked on the floor.
In *that* he heard the hailstones fall,
counted the syllables on his fingers,
and when he got it right,
slapped the bare wood with both palms.
At the sudden sound, the sparrows scared,
the innkeeper's daughter squawked,
and clumsily spilt the tea.

Fortunetelling

Walking by again
the row of star and palm
readers, who would track
and sell me back my future,
I cross Kathmandu's Ratna Park
—bangle and book hawkers,
the hiss of Tibetan fry-bread,
betel juice spat in the dust
—to the bus stop. It's Sunday,
the weekend is over, and back
I go to the monastery-school
to listen to chanted repetitions
of B-I-R-D-Bird.
(Their textbook illuminates the word
with a ruddy North American robin.)

I've been here too long.
The cheap plink of my coins
in the beggar's tin dish,
her halo of heat-slow flies,
her eyes cast over like fried egg yolks,
are words and no longer hurt
me except in retrospect.
Only *wound* is *blessing*,
in Old English a bloody
consecration of the altar,
stone and earth turned temple.
And I know my heart no longer
bleeds. Intact, untouched.

The bus is a VW van,
stripped of all but the driver's chair
and two nailed-down benches.
Usually the driver jammed us in
so tight those standing
couldn't fall. But today,

46

late as I am,
the van is oddly almost empty
—one bench crammed hip to elbow,
the other bare except for her,
a woman, ordinary with her torn
sari and market bag of carrots and mangoes.
No one dares go near her.
And though she wears no bell nor
label, still I can tell
by the others' kept distance,
even if noncontagious,
the woman is a leper.

There are no seats left
on the side that looks
safe and no straps
to hold in the middle alone
so I board and sit not right
beside her but near
as courtesy will allow.

I love my horror, the shiver
and smell of her ripe fruit,
the dangerous
balk and swerve of the bus.
Once I even, as if by
accident, brush her silk
skirts. She shies from
my blue-eyed sidelong glances,
counts and recounts her five
lace-topped carrots. I wonder
if she lives by herself,
if the numbing of leprosy
dulls an easy appetite for
and fear of those who know
and would retell her future.

There's not a mark on her.
Her only scars

are wrinkles and the pock
where a nose-ring hole has half
grown back. Did she sell
the jewel that once
shone there? Surely
she has no daughter in need
of gifts toward a bridal dowry,
has never felt an infant's
(from Latin, not yet speaking)
miraculous, reflexive
grasp of her finger
in its small fist.

She must be childless,
I think, like me. And so now
full of self-pity,
and for the first time
afraid, I love her,
and remember seven years must pass
before I know if the touch of her
dress has infected
me. It takes that long
for the contagion to touch the nerves.

III

After the Annunciation

1.
I did not believe. My body,
clean beneath the robes, was touched
by no more than his cool words.
The stranger's fingers never brushed
my wrist, my cheek, my thigh—but
Beloved, he said. Don't be afraid.
Outside beyond my father's land,
the dusty row of terebinth trees,
Joseph's saw whined and rasped
through a thick hunk of wood.
Now I should draw my betrothed some water,
I thought. Now I should go.
Beloved, the stranger spoke again.

If I felt more than fear
what harm is there in that?
Later that night while the others slept
I held my own two breasts in my hands.
This is my body, I thought, my life.

2.
Like a girl I lie alone until sunrise.
First there are locusts,
then fewer, then silence.
A small room of silence.
My body begins to prove its burden.
What is spirit that its child
should ride so heavy beneath my dress?

Joseph already gone by daylight,
I eat my bread and fish alone.
Once as I ate I heard the roadside beggars

chant. They sang and beat
their bowls with spoons.
It was a long time before they passed.

Most days I've spent in prayer
begging for a word, a sign.
Last night my prayers were answered.
In a dream the spirit came again.
With his fleshy thumb he smeared
a dark line along my skin.
It begins at my navel.
It ends where I woke.

3.
We have left the land of my father—
the gardens and vines, sheep like scattered
melon seeds across the western highlands—
and walked south to the land of my husband.
Early on we entered a wood.
The rough and resinous
bark of the trees, the birds,
and under a bolt of sun, flowering mint.
I was content just to breathe.
Joseph cut down the catmint stalks
and we chewed on the leaves
as we walked.
    We joined
the great trunk road to Jerusalem.
We passed the Philistine plains
where hot wide squares of barley
whir and spit with locusts,
came down through the dry olive orchards
into this chalky land
where the soil is useless dust and lime
and not only women breathe
through a veil.
    After the chalk, though—
I've seen the blot of walls

and soldiers' towers ahead—Jerusalem
lies, Jerusalem, city of the child's birth.
It must be so, tomorrow, I think
on the public straw of another inn,
shadows posed on the walls like puppets.
My body will act. It must be so.
And the secret I've hidden will fall
headlong, breathless into the world.
My night and day will be over.
Strangers will clean my thighs.

Daughters of Jerusalem

Luke 23:28-30

Meanwhile there are dates and milk
on the table, bowls, a jar of oil,
the high ecstatic voice of a child
chasing sparrows from the doorstep.
A woman shakes fleas
from her family's blankets.
Another trims the charred lantern wick.
Her unborn child is quick in her body.
When late this afternoon the sky
turns mottled dark and yellow,
the women will tether the milk goats
and call the children in under the roofs.
As she stands in the doorway waiting
for the cold slant of rain,
a woman thinks, how lucky
we've not yet sheared the lambs.
She thinks of the panicked
bleats on the hill, the raw curls,
the knife and the flesh,
and then later the baled wool
hung from the rafters to ooze
its slow fragrant lanolin wealth.
How lucky, she thinks, and latches the door.

Winter Apples

A stranger in Leningrad,
I walked alone all morning
through cold, quiet streets given
to gusts of rain and Baltic
air, past a cheap cafe so
crowded the windows had fogged
with laughter and steaming tea,
into a grocery shop stocked
with purple-shouldered turnips,
cider, and shiny, salted
black loaves—the dense, beery rye
I always taste in the words
bread of sorrow. Outside snow
began to fall.
                        Once I saw
a black-and-white photograph
of St. Petersburg before
the war: a man is leading
a swayback cab horse out of
the unexposed dark into
falling snow and light. A loaf
of black bread is held against
the rabbi's chest. His ungloved hand
rests on the mare's bridle.
Snow melts in his beard. At home,
he imagines, his wife just
then is pouring out glasses
of buttermilk for the girls.
A dish of fried onions and
apples graces the table.
He sees that lights are burning
late in the soldiers' barracks,
too late—a sign of danger.
And he smells still the malt-washed
crust of the bread in the clean
snow, the horse's steamy breath . . .

I think that night, the straw-ticked
mattress prickling his side,
he will turn down the blankets
to watch his wife's body sleep.
The storm has quit. In her stall,
the mare startles at the noise
of mice scratching for hayseed
in the manger.
                    I bought the bread
and returned through the wet snow.
On the curb a fruit vendor
halved an apple, pared away
the wormholes for a schoolgirl.
I thought she was his daughter.
He put half in her satchel,
half in her red mitten, then
gave me one, too. Even though
the apples were tight-knuckled
fists. Even though the hard
flesh was so white and so cold
it would make my teeth just ache.

For Love of Nina Ruth

Finally last night, under the weight
of its own fruit, the apple's limb
just broke. Not our tree, not our
allegorical problem, and yet
I feel responsible. Every afternoon
for weeks, ever since the tree's green
fruit swelled up ripe, red, heavy
across the alleyway, it's looked
as if the apple's branches strained,
leaning closer to the undergrowth of wild
purple asters mixed with goldenrod—
flowers I've stopped daily to admire.
Daily too I've gazed appraising up
into the tree, gaudy with its overload
of pucker-bottomed Delicious fruit,
and gauged, laying odds, how long
the limbs would hold unpropped. Now
a hundred apples lie there decomposing
in the rough. The others still alive and hanging
go untouched—even those in easy reach—
gathering momentum for the fall.
I should steal the apples outright
or else that fruit and even the overgenerous
tree are only a gorgeous waste.

I reach down and take an apple.
Bluish red, the color rose madder, it looks
perfect and yet, hot with the work
of decay and October sun, it gives
at my slight touch. And underneath—
where the apple had met the earth—
a fragrant fontanelle of rot.
I crack the skin-seal with a thumbnail,
sink my thumbs into the soft stem end,
and yank, twisting, to break the apple in half.
Its white meat is stained red

at the skin and umber around the bruise
and seedy core, its womb-shaped heart.

I held a friend's infant daughter, Nina Ruth,
last night till her slack, sleeping weight
had my unaccustomed arms aching.
It was good. We were alone and so
I sang to her in whatever music came to mind—
a lullaby, a mantra I had learned and thought
forgotten in Nepal, words in a jumble—
"Further in Summer than the Birds,"
"The world is too much with us late and soon"
and so on. Words were all the same to her.
She slept through everything until at last
she woke hungry. Then no words would slow
her cries, no music distract her fear.
And the bottle was no good either.
It was wrong and rocking wouldn't right it.
In hope or from despair (we were both afraid)
I undid my shirt to offer the child my breast,
and I brushed her cheek to turn her head,
a trick I learned from a book.
Almost instantly her crying stopped,
she sighed, and began to suck. Dreamy-
eyed, she gazed up, returned to bliss
for a moment. She sucked hard and then
harder. Then she howled and who could blame her?
So back and forth we went between the bottle
and my live but empty breast. Practical child,
she took what she could from each.

On Courtesy

By the protocol of tides—so stately
a slosh of all the world's water—the Sand
Point salt marsh brims and empties, fills
and bottoms out. The tern dives accordingly.
According to not just the terns' fine tradition but also
to what is most practical: where the water
flows, so go the fish. And yet
as if witness to a miracle or crime
you will watch for hours, binoculars trained
as the bird banks, folds its wings, and drops—
a pretty sight once, twice, even three or five times,
but *your* interest is excessive or, more
likely, feigned. What are you trying to prove?

All day the sun, in summer's blurred white
glare, proceeds across the sky. All night
the moon in an aura of cloud will follow. Thus
the tides and rising surf, their rhythm unbroken
by complaint, apology, our little traumas.
They keep to their decorous shiftlessness
no matter what. I too would scorn polite
talk—the nods and the careful self-revelations
over the lips of wine goblets   except that courtesy
is what is most practical and often what works.
That bird is an emblem of nothing but work.
The miracle is not its resurrection from
deep under but its purposeful, head-first return.

Linda Turner

1. Approaches Her Thirty-fifth Birthday

The white sheets, the wide bed lying beneath her like water—
how, she imagines, would she appear
now to her husband, her slack limbs
open in a big crooked X? Old Bluebeard's

treasure: X marks the spot? Pauline in peril tied up
and down to the train tracks and desperate
for her loyal Royal Mountie?
a photo captioned . . . *Exposé* in boldface?

She toys idly with such silly notions. She knows to her
husband she'd look naked, that is, late.
"Hey Lazybones," he'd say smiling.
Linda makes no move to rise, dress, reclaim her

sensible version of loveliness. *Ah loveliness. Ah
youth* . . . she sighs theatrically, posing.
The static of his shower stops,
and matter-of-fact, unknowingly graceful,

she rises thinking of coffee and whether
her white cotton blouse has been ironed.

2. Recalls Her Autumn Wedding Day

The lilac at her window has exhaused its first loveliness.
Leaves are its one ornament now, but of leaves
it sports at least three thousand, all as close
to identical as the pearls her grandmother chose to leave

"for Linda's wedding day." As the executor read, Linda's
mother looked choked up and squeezed her daughter's hand.
Moments later, emotions mastered, Mother
whispered in her ear, "Cultured, perfect, worth three grand."

Linda did, and not from duty, wear the pearls on her wedding
    day—
her something old, her one ornament, chaste
as the Congregational church. It wasn't an afternoon in May,
womanly lilacs lush in her arms, but chaste

October and a florist's concoction of ivy and crysanthemums.
Ever since with unconfessed nostalgia, she has loved
the bitter, spinster scent of mums,
loved and longed for lilacs even as she loved.

3. Linda Turner's Happy Marriage

Evenings after work, cold evenings out on the flagstone
    terrace,
Linda sometimes lapses into eloquent revery.
"Remember?" she begins in a dreamy, distracted tone.
Her husband, so signaled, tips back his head

and listens to their lives transformed to fiction.
She loves his full attention, loves his praise—
the way he always says she could and should
compose a novel. Tonight the setting sun

clears a neighbor's oak and dawns upon
their fence of morning glories just as Linda
is recounting all the ironies of their wedding day.
Ah, she thinks, and interrupts the plot.

"Look" and as they look the flowers open
slowly, blue. A melody that's plagued
her all day long comes then with lyrics—unbidden.
Linda sings, "You can't hurry love. No . . ."

At a loss, she falters, but her husband
takes it up and sings for her the doxology
of their separate childhoods. The sun
goes finally down on Maple Street. The swallows

cross and twitter, twitter and cross in the blue
dusk of Linda's charmed middle age.

4. The Trinity Church Bells Start in on Six. Linda Turner
Wakes.

She contemplates the snow falling past a streetlight.
Glad in the solitude of her lone wakefulness—
everyone, her husband, even the Sunday
paperboy (apparently) is sleeping, Linda pulls on

slick-soled boots and takes to the unplowed streets.
She runs three steps, skids far on her heels,
as far as a child could slide. Then unlike
a child, herself as a happy, unsatisfied child,

she slows. She strolls beneath the trees and storm.

Linda would enjoy the street's snow-baffled music—
the creak of a burdened sycamore, the purr
of a voltage transformer, distant dogs—except
for the usual, nagging desire. Children. A daughter,

perhaps, in red woolen mittens, dragging
a red-runnered sled. And when the imagined
girl hurls her reckless self and sled downhill?
What if she falls? frets our melodramatic

Linda, stalled in the snow and lonely now
for a shadow girl and a pair of red mittens.

IV

Idleness

Yesterday a cardinal and two house sparrows
Clung to a dried-up, used hollyhock
stalk I'd been too lazy to cut.
Its double Chinese flowers had bloomed
A yard of fat pink in July and passed
Into autumn's drowse neglected

Until I saw the birds, swayed with the stalk,
Unconcerned in the wind, eating seed
I hadn't thought to imagine. Once,
At a gust, the cardinal spread her wings
To baffle the blow, and, animate flower,
She steadied the stalk for all three.

Prosperity

Plum-black olives,
plucked on the sly from the Ronda
trees, stain our hands. Stolen,
uncured, they are alum
and red inside, flesh packed hard
around the stone. No wonder no birds
swarm the untended, abandoned-to-wind groves.
And the bitterness figures. *Crime doesn't pay.*
Cheaters don't prosper, you say like my brother
when some dozen years ago
he and I and Liz and Eric and Lynnie
played softball in the street.
Out, he yelled. *Safe*, I yelled,
and my ghost is safe at third, too.
Night, it went like that,
after night, among the murmur and blue
glow of the neighbors' TVs.
Here it's October and in the verging
mountains, cold. Downslope
sage, artemisia, tarnished silver
olive leaves, and it is
peaceful. After a while stars
replace the lights back in town.
This is happiness I think
—solitude and still
the sound of your breath,
the forms of the full trees gone,
in temporary dark, leaving and having
left, returning. Every night another
pitch and near miss. Cheaters do prosper.
Tomorrow we'll wake in these fields,
frost in our hair,
for one more day in love.
We'll stash our sleeping bags
in some dry culvert and again
by the same road,

walk back to town for breakfast
while behind us, Gypsies
will be shaking the olives from the trees
and filling their skirts
with the fallen fruit.
If they miss a few, so what?

Windfall

The sky is flush
against the ground, copper roofs, trees,
struggling onion grass, and hyacinths—
no gaps, slack space, no
transition from blue air to density
to flesh. Today
there is no discernible
hierarchy of being. Grackles
in tacking against the wind,
turn edgewise and nearly disappear,
turn back and are solid birds with an appetite
for gravel.
       God, where does it say
that such days must be so rare?
There was one, another, Bonnie was there.
We grilled veal on sticks with wild sage,
there was bread and the sky
trailed its blue
scrim against our upturned faces.
                  But
it's not just love.
You know when the sun
streaks its wide ray of almost solid
light through from behind the clouds,
glory, they call it,
a correspondence of angels if angels
are light—
       then too the sensation
of unmediated sky, cobalt to cornflower.
But it's not just celestial.
I walked cold through New Hampshire orchards knowing
our friendship was broken for good.
A white mare in the snow, blue
in the shade and sun going down, stood
pawing for windfall apples. Her prints,
her way through the snow,

led over the rise to a row
of birches.
                    Sunstruck torn bark
and the raw twigs of the growing trees.
Enough, I thought then, enough
that those white trees hold up their white limbs.
But it was not enough
till the sky came down past the stars,
close and ice and, above all, present.

This is an Ode

This is an ode to the noise of fire.

This is an ode to three black jackdaws.
This is an ode to the reeled snail shells plowed white in the
earth like salt.
This is an ode to sour wine.
This is an ode to the olives mulled in garlic, bay, sage, and
brine.

This is an ode to the sage, growing.
This is an ode to the stumble-clanked bells, the goat-cropped
grass, the goats going down on their knees.
This is an ode to the wind's wide arc.
This is an ode to the gaps, black among the blurring stars.

This is an ode to the glacier-scored horizon.
This is an ode to the pollen-streaked throats of the autumn
crocus.
This is an ode to saffron.
This is an ode to lime, dust. pumice, mica.

This is an ode to the void-place, the threshing floor, the or-
chestra.
This is an ode to flour.
This is an ode to the wool tufts snagged on the thistles.
This is an ode to the random, wilding clouds.

This is an ode to smoke, the city, Montale, Hopkins, lemons,
air, thirst, cold.
This is an ode to paper and gorsewood and juniper.
This is an ode to wooden matches.
This is an ode to the intimate sulfur—struck.

This is an ode to the blue gasp, the flare, and the ashes.
This is an ode to cold ashes.

Morning

Before I read the words,
I heard *morning* doves, low
    Voice of the early, not-yet-falling

Rain, dove-gray and white-barred feathers,
Quick, dovetailed wings. I thought
    Their oohs and ahs as gentle a song

As any conceivable dove might sing.
But is the call of a *mourning*
    Dove song? Can this grief be made beautiful?

You're dead. That's not pretty.
But I woke early into the long
    Dusk before morning

This morning and listened for
Those birds you said you loved.
    And listened to those birds you loved.

March Snow

Yesterday in the ice-grizzled hemlocks,
Beyond a natural palisade of snow-
Broken birch, I walked out till dusk
And stood there long enough to see the sparrows,
Hunched on the evergreen branches, quiver.
A rabbit, incautious, white except for one
Dangerous tuft of unmolted summer fur,
Loped slow across my path and was gone.
When snow began, I heard the regular tick
Of its falling—everywhere touched at once.
I'd have lain down under the hemlocks
And slept to disappear, but snow's no penance
Or white, worldly absolution. It's snow.
A March snow that's already rain at our window.

Rain

Our windows are rinsed with a cold autumn rain.

The white noise composed of its constancy
almost obscures a trio of carolling dogs,
someone's reluctant pick-up engine,
and the little racket my rocking chair makes on the floor.

The rain has rained slowly all afternoon long.

On the neighbors' front porch, their fat ten-year-old
    daughter,
who is just as afraid of her classmates'
jibes as she is of her parents' fists, rocks
the porch swing back and forth. I think

—despite the gray yards of raindrops between us—

I can see her singing. And why not?
Yesterday, too, I noticed her walking
—late to avoid her tormentors—to school.
She carried books and an open umbrella.

The streets were slick with rain and rain-downed leaves.

The sky showed only enough unravelling cloud
to prove its blue clarity. The girl—
I don't know her name—suddenly danced,
twirling her pink-striped umbrella

as if she wished there were rain like this rain,
rain enough to dim the distracting world around her joy.

Knowledge

for Clare

I would deny myself the lilacs,
the curses and blessings of the wind,
the seven flowering apple trees
of my childhood, and the ocean
if that would protect you.

What is it I wish to protect you
from? It can't be sorrow for sorrow
is knowledge, and what else is there
but knowledge? It was winter the night
you were born from my body, solemn,

eyes open and unblinking.
You were not afraid,
though I almost wished you were,
I wanted so much for my
touch to comfort and to protect you.

October First

It is singed, the air; the ash is green;
the oak bends its penitential head
and you, Clare, unencumbered,
laugh at the cold antics of the wind.

You carry no ballast of flowers,
no cargo of talismanic stones
thumb-worn in your coat pocket.
Every sheaf of opening

roses wakes in you the same
laugh, the same true love so easily
distracted—by more roses,

ragged sky, or a dried-up oak leaf's
wind-roving shadow. Because
to you the world is only the world.

Birds of the Air

for Eric

The young swallows are learning grace
this morning by failing. I mean their rough,
difficult flight, the way they flap
too much, not trusting the thin air
to hold them, the way all four
fledglings refuse to use the wind,
believing, is failing. Twice the birds
have hit the window glass and almost
dropped, stunned. Easy flight isn't natural.
The knack of a barn swallow's quick
and accurate, almost-to-falling glide
is not, as I'd have thought, inborn
intelligence, a sort of ether
that fills a barn swallow's hollow bones.

Simplicity is the achievement. Consider the elegant
parent swallows that skim out low
across the marsh—salt spray rose, muck,
and blueberry scrub, reeds and tidal creek—
in effortless, unerring flight, hunting.
They are willing to ride the air—now—
but like their young when they were young
they must have flapped, toiled, and flustered,
have failed, too. Every muscle resisting
the pull of what pulled them.
How did they learn that graceful
giving in, that belief in invisible air?
It must have been exigency—fatigue,
gravity, hunger, sheer desperate hunger.

Choosing Happiness

for Bob and Margie

         The summer
river slows between its banks
—one sloping sand fraught only
by killdeer whose cries are fair
descriptions of the beauty
that is solitude; the other
cut sheer, and overhung with oak
in full leaf, lush, and toppling
gradually forward.
                 Downstream
canoeing is allowing
the current to do the work,
steering only to avoid
the sandbars, rocks, and deadfalls.
We balance our paddles
across the hull, lean back.
                 This,
we say, *is the life*, meaning
the good, the happy life. As
if happiness were just this
effortless, affordable.
Just this easy to accept.
Alarmed, a gray heron lifts
from awkwardness into flight.
There are dragonflies, finches,
a catfish, gnawed to the gills
and washed clean. Minnows of such
clear new flesh, we can see right
through to the intimate bone.
Then from the willow grass, rough
with crickets, we startle up
indigo buntings.
             We can
choose to call this happiness
life. Claim it, as the river

lays claim to the bankside oaks.
By continuing. By not
refusing.
              At dusk we share
bread, fish, smoked cheese, tomatoes,
good bourbon, and a driftwood
fire. *Stars, owl, wind*. The moment.
And its passing. That fear.

About the Author

Jennifer Atkinson received a Pushcart Prize for poetry in 1988 and one for an essay in 1989. A graduate of the Iowa Writers' Workshop, she presently serves as the editor of *River Styx* and teaches at Washington University. Her poems have appeared in *Poetry, Prairie Schooner,* the *Cincinnati Poetry Review, The Reaper*, and *Sonora Review*.